D1222993

JOHN HELIKER

SELF PORTRAIT. *1959. Oil. 24 x 20. Collection of Armand G. Erpf.*

By Lloyd Goodrich and Patricia FitzGerald Mandel

JOHN HELIKER

Published for the
Whitney Museum of American Art
by Frederick A. Praeger, Publishers
New York • Washington • London

Published in the United States of America in 1968
by FREDERICK A. PRAEGER, Inc., Publishers
111 Fourth Avenue, New York, N. Y. 10003
77-79 Charlotte Street, London W. 1, England
Library of Congress Catalog Card Number: 68-25639

Designed by Museum Planning, Inc.

Printed in the United States of America
by Publishers Printing — Admiral Press, New York

JOHN HELIKER

In a statement of his ideas on art, in 1954, John Heliker wrote that modern artists from Cézanne on had created "a whole new conception of what painting is (though in truth, a very ancient conception): the idea of a painting not as a literal transcription of natural objects telling a story, but as a unity, a microcosmos, in which each element, including the subject, plays an equal and significant role, so that the painting contains a message of order far beyond literal interpretation of objects. Nor does this preclude the presence of warm human elements, of drama or of serenity." This conception of the basic nature of painting has governed Heliker's work since his artistic beginnings in the 1930's.

Heliker has always been an individualist, expressing himself in primarily personal terms. His art is based on nature and his subjective responses to nature, but it speaks in the physical language of form and color rather than of naturalistic representation. His development has been highly individualistic. A few years of rather fragmentary art school study in his youth had far less effect on him than his years-long direct communion with nature, and his constant search for the forms that would most clearly and exactly embody his sensations and emotions. A thoughtful, knowledgeable artist, fully aware of other art, past and present, he has used the explorations of modern art without being strongly influenced by any particular school or creed. Through the years his style has passed through varying degrees of abstraction but has never become purely abstract. From the first it has been based on design — on the physical structure of the work of art, its form, color, line and movement, and the total harmony achieved by sensitive command of the interrelations and interplay of all these elements.

Drawing has always played an essential part in Heliker's work. "Drawing for me is never subsidiary to painting," he wrote recently. "It is a very intense part of my work. For me, drawing is almost a daily experience — a means of exploring my ideas and giving structure to them." It was in drawing that he first found his individual expression. His early drawings were of the life he knew best, that of the country — farm scenes with a Bruegel-like peasant flavor that now seems oddly at variance with the refinement of his mature work. These drawings were almost entirely in line, with little concern for tone or texture — an uncompromising linear style that sometimes tended to be labored and wooden. The bulky, awkward figures showed a striving for mass and volume, and a strong idiosyncratic character of form, which also marked his few figure paintings of the time. His landscape drawings, on the other hand, had a sensitivity of line that foretold the linear skill of his later oils.

His most fully realized early paintings were landscapes, revealing a preference for the solitary and serene aspects of nature. "I have found the Vermont countryside especially hospitable to my painting activities," he wrote in the mid-1940's. "Its blue hills and quiet villages, its magnificent rock formations, have given me the sort of material I like to work with. . . . I find myself more at home in the 'little world' of the farm — I feel free to work slowly there — where one is consistently aware of fundamentals." This strain of quiet idyllic poetry was combined with a feeling for the structure of the earth, for the rugged forms of mountains, cliffs and rocks — a structural awareness related to his youthful and continuing interest in Cézanne. And in these landscapes Heliker revealed himself as a born colorist, using color not only for its own deep-toned harmonies but for its integration with form.

In early visits to Maine, Heliker found another elemental theme, the sea. In his first Maine landscapes the stark forms of this rocky coast were pictured with romantic emotion; the strange dramatic shapes of cliffs and clouds recall Marsden Hartley, and Hartley's great admiration, Albert Ryder. From then on, the sea and the coast were to be constant recurring motifs in Heliker's work, not only in Maine, which has been his summer home since 1958, but in his travels in Italy, Greece and Nova Scotia.

Heliker's early naturalism was never mere representation; the emphasis was always on the forms of nature and their translation into the forms of art. Of a Vermont landscape of 1943 he wrote: "It is a fairly naturalistic presentation; however, my concern was mainly with the organization of the plastic elements." And in a statement in 1954 about his artistic development he said: "I find strong abstract elements and formal relationships in my earliest attempts at painting, no matter how representational they may appear. For even here a certain sense of order, by which I mean a tentative awareness of all the elements in a unified relationship, is evident, even though perhaps minute. It is this element of order that broadens and develops with increasing insight."

So there was underlying consistency in the change that came over his work in the mid-1940's. "Around 1945 and 1946," he later wrote, "I began to explore my 'means' and formal organization more intensely in relation to all elements, and my work became less representational." His first semi-abstract pictures of these years were a continuation of his naturalistic works in their essential content. What was new was a purging of merely representational elements, a freeing of imagery, and a concentration on form. The first fruits of this change were a series of pastels and oils in which the forms were not specifically recognizable, yet retained some of the character of the rocks and trees and driftwood of his early pictures, but now with a sense of images seen in dreams, with haunting associations. But this surrealist phase proved only transitional.

The more permanent transformation came with his visit to Italy in 1948 and 1949, the first of six long Italian sojourns over the next ten years. He soon discovered a deep affinity for that ancient land: the formal beauty of its cities and towns, especially the 12th- and 13th-century Norman-Saracenic architecture of Southern Italy; the warm earth colors of stone, brick and plaster; the land itself, shaped and mellowed by centuries of human cultivation; and the intimate relation between nature and the works of man, so that the towns on their hilltops seem outgrowths of the forms of earth.

Italy's uniquely close relation between the natural and the man-made, between landscape and architecture, formed the central theme of Heliker's Italian paintings. Mostly small in scale (perhaps due to transportation problems), they were considerably nearer abstraction than his American landscapes. They still used recognizable images: towns and buildings, valleys and hills and seacoast. Glimpses of city walls, towers, colonnades, Romanesque arches, were incorporated into complicated patterns resembling mosaic or inlay. The deep variegated color harmonies suggested marble, brick, old masonry, the colors of the earth. But all these echoes of the visual world were subordinated to overall schematic design, purer and more evident than in previous works. Compositions were rectilinear and angular, dominated by the long horizontals of land and sea, broken by subtly related verticals and diagonals. The style was marked by precision and refinement, and sensitive linear definition. The closely-knit planes of varying textures, tones and colors, formed intricate geometrical patterns. All elements were unified into complex interlocked design. But there was nothing dry or sterile in this semi-geometric style; on the contrary, color and tonal values had a new richness and depth. In spite of their modest scale, these Italian paintings were among his most concentrated, fully realized formal creations.

These characteristics continued in his American cityscapes of these years; the towers of Manhattan's bridges recalled those of Italian palazzi. But particularly in his Maine paintings,

PIG STICKING. *1936. Ink. 9⅝ x 12. University of Nebraska Art Galleries.*

the design grew freer. "In Italy," he wrote, "I was much influenced by its architectural beauty, and concerned myself largely with architectural forms. But returning to Maine and its great natural beauty, I was impelled to further exploration: the use of freer forms and curvilinear movement in relation to a somewhat less defined kind of structure." Instead of man-made architecture, he was now occupied with the architecture of the earth — the rock formations of the Maine coast, rugged and at the same time finely sculptured by milleniums of natural forces. The precise interlocked structure continued, but now less rectilinear. There was a growing simplification, and a loosening of the tightly-knit patterns of the Italian pictures. Specific images tended to disappear, and his style approached nearer to abstraction.

About 1955 came changes more basic, appearing particularly in his Maine landscapes. The scale of the paintings grew considerably larger, the design freer, the color lighter and purer. Rectilinear patterning gave way to looser fluid composition, expressive of nature's irregular forms and living movements. Elements were recognizable as trees, rocks, houses, or the sea, but translated into semi-abstract images, pictorial metaphors, and assimilated into overall linear and chromatic designs, interwoven and intricate. There was a new sense of movement and rhythm. Color assumed a larger role, high-pitched and clear, prevailingly cool, with tones of blue, blue-green, pale rose, vermilion and silvery grays that were new in his palette. Often the colors were applied in touches placed side-by-side, not with the methodical impressionist technique of divided tones, but in larger shaped patches of colors playing one against another — warm against cool, positive against neutral, strong against delicate — creating a chromatic vibration over the whole surface. At first sight these canvases might produce an effect of flat arabesques, but as one looks at them, projecting and receding planes emerge, and design as precise as in his geometrical works, but now free-flowing. This new phase might be called semi-abstract impressionism, akin to Marin or to Claude Monet's late works.

Heliker has seldom if ever painted directly from nature. (Many of his drawings are done from nature, but they are independent works, unconnected or only remotely connected with paintings.) Nor does he make studies for his paintings. Writing of his landscapes in 1954, he said: "Before starting to paint I never have a complete result in mind. The basis of subject matter is actual, but my interpretation is free and personal. *Of Maine,* for example, relates to the experience last summer of long walks by the edge of the sea on an island off the coast of Maine; and the painting started with representational cloud and rock shapes which eventually were broken down into the portrayed relationships. Although there remain virtually no objects representing those one might find on this coast, I feel that the painting contains a more intense feeling of the experience than any literal use I might have made of these shapes and forms.

"Though I rarely make a preliminary study in any medium for a painting, I usually spend a good deal of time contemplating the scene from all angles. If I am interested in a specific subject, I go back to it from time to time to try to understand its varying and special qualities and moods. After some especially intense experience in nature, I often take a blank canvas and, with no very specific idea in mind, start to put down a few lines, establish a few shapes and color relationships, until gradually an idea emerges expressive of the experience. Thus a painting is born out of the materials, in the first place, is developed with work and by the process of elimination, and gradually becomes clarified, and I hope, significant in its relationships."

This method has parallels with the instinctivism of the abstract expressionists, for whom the physical materials of painting and their manipulation have much to do with determining the final forms — a process like that of automatic writing. But while Heliker designs as he paints, he still designs — consciously and clearly, and with a dominating desire for order. This sense of order sets him apart from most abstract expressionism. "In recent years," he wrote in 1954, "I have been concerned in my painting with the quality of serenity, which seems to be at variance with much of the current abstract expressionist work. While abstract expressionism seems often to mirror the turmoil and violence

VOYAGE. *1948. Pastel. 13½ x 21.*

STUDY. *1953. Gouache. 20⅝ x 7½. Collection of Mr. and Mrs. Alan L. Washburn.*

of the world today, I choose in my painting to give expression to those aspects of nature which contain an inner sense of harmony."

The last five or six years have brought a new development: a series of interiors, sometimes with figures. These paintings are more representational than those of the preceding decade; the objects and figures are fully recognizable. The style, as in his Italian paintings, is basically rectilinear; but instead of relatively flat patterning, the recent interiors are deliberate constructions in deep space. Walls, stairs, doorways, mantels, tables and chairs are used as elements in three-dimensional construction, stressing straight lines meeting or crossing at sharp angles, creating a rectangular grid in space. This renewed architectonic quality has been accompanied by a notable expansion in range and depth of color — still high-keyed and on the cool side, but with a wider gamut, down to deep notes. In these recent paintings Heliker has achieved a synthesis of the two motivating forces in his art: his search for formal order, and his sense of chromatic and tonal harmony.

LLOYD GOODRICH

In 1940, John Heliker painted *Vermont Farm*. In 1941, he submitted it to the biennial exhibition of the Corcoran Gallery of Art and won the W. A. Clark first prize of $2,000 as well as the Corcoran Gold Medal. Months earlier, the painting, which was only 14 x 20, had been for sale at the Walker Galleries for $125 — with no expressed interest.

The event provided young Heliker — then just over thirty — with sustenance and encouragement for the next years. How acute was his need for encouragement is capsuled in his recollection of the day he learned the news. He had come down to New York from his home in Yonkers, New York, at the request of Maynard Walker, his dealer. Walker was closing his gallery and wanted Heliker to clear out his paintings and drawings. Heliker had no immediate prospects and no idea how to approach another dealer — his association with Walker having

END OF THE ISLAND, CRANBERRY. *1963. Ink. 13½ x 16¾. Collection of Henry Schnakenberg.*

been through the efforts of a friend. He made his way through St. Patrick's parade hilarity to the gallery, where he was overwhelmed by the congratulatory telegram.

With the prize money, Heliker bought a car and went to Vermont, where he rented a farm house in the Winooski Valley, between Plainfield and Marshfield. There he was near his good friend, Carl Ruggles, the composer, who had converted a one-room school house in Arlington into the studio depicted in *Interior,* 1942.

It was natural that Heliker should wish to return to the country once he was able to do as he liked. His life had always been rural. He was born in Yonkers, on January 17, 1909, to John Edward Heliker and Jane MacLaughlin; their first and only child, as another boy did not survive. His father was a stonemason, working with his grandfather, also named John Edward Heliker, in the latter's building firm in Yonkers. Their home was in the country and they "always had a horse and lots of poultry." Heliker recalls with pride how he and his father would bring their prize roosters to be exhibited at Madison Square Garden.

When he was a young man of twenty, his family moved to a farm in Stormville, New York, near Poughkeepsie, where he helped with the daily chores and tended the fields and livestock. His familiarity with farm life is explicit in his early drawings of pig-sticking, butchering, cattle-dealing and wood-cutting. Their sharp Bruegel flavor recalls Heliker's own Dutch ancestry: Jacob Heliker had come from Holland to New Amsterdam in the seventeenth century, settling the land near where Trinity Church now stands.

Heliker's drawings depict faceless country people intent upon their tasks. He records their periphery with great precision: lumber caps, thick-soled farm shoes, wagons, slatted wooden barrels and leafless trees with knobby joints. From the first, he worked in pen, dry-brush and watercolor, occasionally using the blunt end of a match for scrubby textures. These works have a tenderness that disclaims their frequent critical comparison with George Grosz; Heliker's drawings have no "sting."

As a boy of fourteen, Heliker had decided to become an artist. He dropped out of Gorton High School, Yonkers, in his third year to pursue his interest in art. He then started a course in self-instruction requiring daily commuting to the Metropolitan Museum where he looked at and copied paintings. He came to know Cézanne, studying especially two works, then on loan from the Havemeyer Collection, *Portrait of a Man in a Straw Hat* and *Still Life.* At this time he met another young copyist, Arshile Gorky, with whom he discussed art, analyzing the works of Cézanne, Gauguin and Manet.

In January 1927, he entered the Art Students League. His first class was a drawing course with Kimon Nicolaides in which students copied plaster casts of ancient art with particular attention to Nicolaides' stress on contour and gesture. Cézanne had said, "While one paints, one draws"; similarly Nicolaides treated painting as an extension of drawing. Heliker's work has always clearly reflected this primacy of draughtsmanship and the majority of his time at the League was spent studying life drawing with Thomas Hart Benton and Boardman Robinson, as well as Nicolaides, whose influence Heliker feels was greatest. He took only two painting courses, both with Kenneth Hayes Miller, making a total of three months, before he left the League in February 1929 for Stormville.

As he started to come to New York more fre-

STILL LIFE. *1963. Charcoal. 23⅜ x 18⅞. Collection of Mr. and Mrs. Howard N. Berntsen.*

quently, his drawings began to incorporate city scenes: men wielding jackhammers, construction workers relaxing at lunch hour, busy street corners. It was one of these street scenes that attracted the collector Paul Sachs at Heliker's first one-man show at Walker's in October 1936. Other drawings, all modestly priced from $15 to $25, were rapidly acquired by museums throughout the country: the Addison Gallery of American Art, the William Rockhill Nelson Gallery, the University of Nebraska Art Galleries and the San Francisco Museum of Art. Reviews were immediately enthusiastic, comparing him to Bruegel, Daumier, Klee and, most often, Grosz, whom, incidentally, he never met. He was invited to exhibit in the 1937 and 1938 International Watercolor Exhibitions at the Art Institute of Chicago and the Brooklyn Museum, respectively.

It was Heliker's painting that was relatively unknown at the time of the Corcoran prize. He had exhibited oils for the first time, only four months before, in November 1940 at Walker's. His hesitancy in showing them can probably be traced to his short period of study and subsequent isolation. He lacked confidence. He had received some encouragement from Philip Evergood, his supervisor in the WPA easel project which he joined in 1938 when he moved from Stormville to Greenwich Village. Occasionally, he met his monthly quota in the project with a painting, but more usually he submitted drawings. He did a great many drawings at this time—contributing some to *New Masses* and donating others to the loyalist cause in the Spanish Civil War. He remained with the WPA for eighteen months and then, late in 1939, left for Vermont where he painted twenty oils for the forthcoming show, mostly still lifes and landscapes, including *Vermont Farm*.

There was a purity and lack of pretension in Heliker's early painting that served to refresh the jury of the Corcoran Biennial, fatigued with social protest art, on the one hand, and the facile work of the one-time Establishment, on the other. The jury, composed of Francis Chapin, Russell Cowles, Guy Pène du Bois, Alexander James and Franklin C. Watkins, as chairman, choose Heliker as the youngest artist ever to receive the Corcoran Gold Medal. Their decision shook a somnolent art world; "But why?" was the universal query. Honesty of technique and paint quality were among the explanations. The very simplicity of the painting appealed, its honest echo of Cézanne, its warm, resonant colors.

Shortly after winning the prize, Heliker began to exhibit widely. His paintings were included in the Metropolitan Museum's Artists for Victory exhibition, 1942, and in the Whitney Museum's Painters Under Forty, 1943. He exhibited regularly in subsequent Corcoran Biennials and in the Annuals of the Art Institute of Chicago, the Pennsylvania Academy of Fine Arts, the University of Illinois and the Whitney Museum.

By 1949, he won four additional prizes: the Pepsi-Cola "Picture of the Year" in 1946, the Adolph and Clara Obrig prize at the National Academy in 1948, the University of Illinois' purchase award in 1949 and the Prix de Rome from the American Academy in Rome for 1948 and 1949. These awards have continued with a 1957 grant from the National Institute of Arts and Letters and a 1967 Award of Merit from the American Academy of Arts and Letters.

His teaching career was established in the late forties and, curiously enough, revolved around painting, rather than drawing. In 1947, he began teaching at Columbia University where he is now an Associate Professor. The summer before, he had taught at the Colorado Springs Fine Arts Center.

In the early forties, Heliker taught painting at the American People's School in the Bronx, run by the dancers Ruth St. Denis and Ted Shawn. That he would select such a school, concerned with all the fine arts, rather than one solely concerned with painting, reveals the catholicity of his artistic tastes. Heliker is extremely fond of and knowledgeable about music, although he does not play an instrument himself. It was he who instigated the publication of *About Carl Ruggles* written in the forties by his friend Lou Harrison, the composer. Heliker also admires modern dance and, about the same time, designed a mask, based on the bird masks of Haida, North West Indies, for a solo performance by Merce Cunningham. He was close friends with Cunningham and John Cage, the composer, and spent much of his first year abroad in their company.

Heliker left for Naples on the Prix de Rome in the fall of 1948 on the *Vulcania* with Philip Guston who had received the same award. From Naples they went to Rome where they

PORTRAIT. *1967. Red chalk. 10 x 7½.*

shared an immense studio and grew to be good friends. Heliker, however, unhappy in Rome, moved to the then-isolated region of Amalfi and Vietri where he stayed until spring. He met his friends Cage and Cunningham in Sicily for the Spring Festival of the International Society for Contemporary Music, of which he too was a member. There, he was enraptured by Palestrinian mass music in the twelfth-century Monreale cathedral, an experience which later mingled with his keen architectural appreciation to produce *Monreale*. Heliker returned to New York the following fall, by way of Paris, and revisited Italy during each of the five succeeding summers. In 1951, his trip was prolonged by a Guggenheim fellowship.

On these return trips, he sought the sea. He revisited Sicily and Naples and toured Sardinia, tracing D. H. Lawrence's route in *Sea and Sardinia*. He visited Tuscany and the Veneto, delighting in the Palladian villas and medieval towns, particularly Siena and Orvieto. He became intrigued with Italy's reconstruction for he had first arrived just after the war and keenly felt the damage and America's part in it. The rebuilding of the Papal palace in Viterbo and the Temple of Fortuna in Palestrina fascinated him as did the archaeological findings that often accompanied such activities.

His annual visits to Italy stopped with 1954. He has returned only once — in 1957, when he was on his way to Greece, and revisited Naples and cut across southern Italy en route to Delphi and Corinth. Most of his time in Greece was spent near the sea. From Mykonos he wrote to John I. H. Baur, then Associate Director of the Whitney Museum: "The sun is sinking beyond Delos — and this town of Mykonos is cast in a fabulous light. One cannot look at this landscape and disassociate it from its mythological past. It is wonderful, but for some reason, I feel oppressed by it and homesick for Maine."

Thus, Heliker came back to Maine to stay and in 1958 bought an old sea-captain's house on Cranberry Island, near Mt. Desert not far from Marin's Deer Island. He had first visited Maine as a boy of sixteen and retells the journey with high adventure. He had taken the overnight steamer alone from New York to Boston to Bath to Bar Harbor. Later, in the mid-forties, he returned to Bar Harbor and Penobscot Bay and, in the fifties, moved to the lighthouse on the Bay that he had depicted in *Driftwood,* some ten years earlier.

In 1966, Heliker received an honorary degree from Colby College for his "success in translating the scenery of our State of Maine into artistic expression." He loves Maine, "the coastal landscape, the proximity to the sea, the light, the outlying islands, the unending pound of the sea and the rocks at its edge."

The uninterrupted stretch of summers has led Heliker toward introspection. His paintings are increasingly concerned with interiors and the placement of objects and figures within them. This recent preoccupation extends his natural predisposition for still life into another dimension, that of space. It is the objects that fill that space that concern him. Heliker is most himself with specifics. His Flemish fondness for detail has moved from the genre of Bruegel to the quietude of Terborch. He loves a certain bouquet of flowers, a certain cat, a certain kettle, a certain bowl of peaches and, like Morandi, whom he so admires, he makes poetry of the commonplace.

PATRICIA FITZ GERALD MANDEL

SELECTED BIBLIOGRAPHY

The place of publication is New York unless otherwise stated.

STATEMENTS BY JOHN HELIKER

Art USA Now, v. 1, 1962. Edited by lee Nordness, text by Allen S. Weller, p. 184.

Contemporary American Painting, (later Contemporary American Painting and Sculpture), University of Illinois, Urbana, 1951, p. 186; 1953, p. 188; 1955, p. 205; 1961, p. 80.

The Encyclopaedia Britannica Collection of Contemporary American Painting, written and edited by Grace Pagano, Chicago, 1946, p. 55.

Nature in Abstraction, written and edited by John I. H. Baur, Whitney Museum of American Art, 1958, p. 7.

The New Decade, edited by John I. H. Baur, Whitney Museum of American Art, 1955, p. 42.

BOOKS (GENERAL)

American Painting Today, edited by Nathaniel Pousette-Dart, 1956, p. 60. 1 il.

Art USA Now, v. 1, 1962. Edited by lee Nordness, text by Allen S. Weller, "Heliker" by Mariah E. Steinberg, p. 182-185. 5 il., 2 por.

Baur, John I. H.: *Nature in Abstraction,* 1958, p. 7, 70. 1 il.

Drawings by American Artists, selected and edited by Norman Kent, 1947, p. 76-77. 1 il.

The Encyclopaedia Brittanica Collection of Contemporary American Painting, written and edited by Grace Pagano, Chicago, 1946, p. 55. 1 il.

Goodrich, Lloyd and Baur, John I. H.: *American Art of Our Century,* 1961, p. 186. 1 il.

Maine and Its Role in American Art, edited by Gertrud A. Mellon and Elizabeth P. Wilder, 1963, p. 162-63, 171. 2 il.

Ritchie, Andrew Carnduff: *Abstract Painting and Sculpture in America,* 1951, p. 151. 1 il.

Who's Who in American Art, 1940, p. 293.

EXHIBITION CATALOGUES

ONE-MAN EXHIBITIONS

John Heliker, Recent Paintings, Department of Art, Queens College, 1961.

Paintings, Watercolors, Drawings and Collages by John Heliker, Storm King Art Center, 1965.

PERIODICALS

AMERICAN ARTIST

v. 19, Sept. 1955, p. 37-40, 69. Carole E. Foeller: "Evolution of a Poet-Painter." 6 il, 1 por.

v. 24, June 1960, p. 34. Peter Pollack: "Fifteen Self-Portraits by American Artists." 1 il.

AMERICAN MAGAZINE OF ART (LATER MAGAZINE OF ART)

v. 29, Dec. 1936, p. 831-832. Howard Devree: "Sculpture and Drawings at Walkers." 1 il.

v. 34, March 1941, p. 134. "Pictures of People." 1 il.

v. 34, April 1941, p. 160-161. Forbes Watson: "Alive or Dead." 1 il.

v. 34, Oct. 1941, p. 421. "Sketches for Collectors." 1 il.

v. 41, Nov. 1948, p. 263. "John Heliker." 2 il.

ART DIGEST (LATER ARTS DIGEST, ARTS, AND ARTS MAGAZINE)

v. 15, Nov. 15, 1940, p. 19. "Heliker's Substance." (In "Fifty-Seventh Street in Review"). 1 il.

v. 15, April 1, 1941, p. 12, 25. "Corcoran Biennial Reflects Trends of Living American Painting." 1 il.

v. 19, April 1, 1945, p. 60. Jo Gibbs: "John Heliker, in Latest Work, Forges Ahead." 1 il.

v. 22, Feb. 1, 1948, p. 20. Alonzo Lansford: "Drawings at the National Academy." 1 il.

v. 22, April 1, 1948, p. 11. Jo Gibbs: "The Left and the Right Meet on Walls of National Academy." 1 il.

v. 23, Oct. 1, 1948, p. 18. Jo Gibbs: "Heliker, Rome-Bound, Exhibits Abstractions." 1 il.

v. 23, March 1, 1949, p. 9-10. Arthur Millier: "Illinois, Leaning to Left, Presents Second Painting Survey." 1 il.

v. 24, Sept. 15, 1950, p. 13. Doris Brian: "How New Britain Built a Collection and Housed It." 1 il.

v. 25, April 15, 1951, p. 17. Mary Cole: "Heliker's Rectangles." 1 il.

v. 27, Oct. 1, 1952, p. 14. "Circuit in the Southeast." 1 il.

v. 28, June 1, 1954, p. 21-22. A.N.: "John Heliker." 1 il.

v. 31, May 1957, p. 49. Elizabeth Pollet: "John Heliker." (In "In the Galleries"). 1 il.
v. 34, May 1960, p. 58. Sidney Tillim: "John Heliker." (In "In the Galleries"). 1 il.
v. 38, Sept. 1964, p. 71. Vivien Raynor: "John Heliker."

ART NEWS

v. 35, Oct. 31, 1936, p. 18. Martha Davidson: "Sturdy Drawings and Watercolors by Heliker." 1 il.
v. 39, Nov. 16, 1940, p. 12. Jeannette Lowe: "Objective Variety by John Heliker."
v. 41, Jan. 1-14, 1943, p. 12, 34. Alfred M. Frankfurter: "The Artists for Victory Exhibition." 1 il.
v. 44, March 1-14, 1945, p. 13. "Accent on Youth in Worcester's U.S. Review." 1 il.
v. 44, April 1-14, 1945, p. 6. "John Edward Heliker." (In "The Passing Shows"). 1 il.
v. 50, May 1951, p. 46. Henry McBride: "Heliker's conscience."
v. 53, Summer 1954, p. 72. Lawrence Campbell: "John Heliker." (In "Reviews and previews").
v. 63, Summer 1964, p. 14. Thomas Neumann: "John Heliker." (In "Reviews and previews").
v. 66, May 1967, p. 13. Marcia Tucker: "John Heliker's." (In "Reviews and previews").

NEW MASSES

March 22, 1938. "Relief Drawings by John Heliker."

PICTURES ON EXHIBIT

May 1951. Review of Heliker Show at Kraushaar.
May 1957. A. N.: "John Heliker." 1 il.
May 1967. Alan P. Wallach: "John Heliker." p. 12, 14. 1 il.

TIME

March 31, 1941. "Bid: $2,000; Asked $125."
May 15, 1964. Review of Heliker's Exhibition at Kraushaar.
May 5, 1967. "John Heliker."

NEWSPAPERS

CHICAGO SUN-TIMES

Feb. 7, 1954. Frank Holland: "Club Shows Easterners' Fine Works."

NEW YORK HERALD TRIBUNE

Oct. 25, 1936. Carlyle Burrows: "John Heliker."
Nov. 17, 1940. Carlyle Burrows: "John Edward Heliker."
March 20, 1941. "John E. Heliker Wins Corcoran Art Show Prize."
April 18, 1945. Review of Show at Kraushaar
Oct. 17, 1948. Review of Show at Kraushaar.
April 8, 1951. "Abstract Perceptions."
May 16, 1954. Review of Show at Kraushaar.
April 28, 1957. "New Works of Heliker."
March 20, 1960. Review of Show at Kraushaar.

THE NEW YORK JOURNAL AMERICAN

Nov. 17, 1940. Margaret Breuning: "John Edward Heliker."

NEW YORK POST

Oct. 24, 1936. Jerome Klein: "Heliker is the name."

NEW YORK SUN

Oct. 24, 1936. Henry McBride: Review of Walker Exhibition. 1 il.
April 8, 1945. Review of Heliker Show at Kraushaar. 1 il.
Oct. 10, 1948. Henry McBride: "Kraushaar Gallery."

THE NEW YORK TIMES

Oct. 25, 1936. Howard Devree: Review of Heliker Exhibition at Walkers.
March 20, 1941. "Works of New York Artists Take Awards in American Oil Painting." 1 il.
April 8, 1945. Review of Heliker Show at Kraushaar.
Oct. 10, 1948. "Two in Process."
Oct. 17, 1948. "Fantasy by a Contemporary." 1 il.
April 8, 1951. "Interpreted Anew." 1 il.
May 12, 1954. Howard Devree: "John Heliker."
May 16, 1954. "Urban Impressions in Shows." 1 il.
April 28, 1957. Review of Heliker Show at Kraushaar.
March 16, 1960. Dore Ashton: "Art: Tradition-Directed." 1 il.
April 22, 1967. Hilton Kramer: "John Heliker."
Dec. 17, 1967. John Canaday: "The Whitney: Not Much Luck In the Bushes."

NEW YORK WORLD-TELEGRAM (LATER WORLD JOURNAL TRIBUNE)

March 22, 1941. Emily Genauer: "The Trend of American Painting As Reflected in Corcoran Show." 1 il.
April 21, 1967. Emily Genauer: "John Heliker."

WASHINGTON POST

March 23, 1941. Alice Graeme: "Biennial Art Show Opens at Corcoran."

ILLUSTRATIONS

SPRING LANDSCAPE. *1943. Oil. 25 x 30. Collection of Mr. and Mrs. Olin J. Stephens II.*

DRIFTWOOD. *1945. Oil. 40 x 30. Collection of Mr. and Mrs. Meyer P. Potamkin.*

MAINE COAST, *1944. Oil. 25 x 34. Atlanta University.*

IMMERSION. *1947. Oil. 29½ x 21½. The New Britain Museum of American Art.*

24

MONREALE. *1950. Oil. 28 x 22. Philadelphia Museum of Art.*

OF MAINE. *1953. Oil. 15¾ x 28½. Whitney Museum of American Art.*

HARLEM RIVER. *1954. Oil. 12½ x 25¼. Collection of Mr. and Mrs. Bernard Heineman, Jr.*

STILL LIFE. *1956. Oil. 20⅝ x 12½. Wadsworth Atheneum.*

WHITE ROCKS, NOVA SCOTIA. *1955. Oil. 13½ x 24½. Mrs. S. M. Barnes Roby.*

EAST RIVER. *1954. Oil. 16 x 24. Collection of Mr. and Mrs. Olin J. Stephens II.*

KITCHEN INTERIOR. *1965. Oil. 42 x 32. Collection of Mr. and Mrs. Morris Smoler.*

INTERIOR. *1961. Oil. 20 x 18¼. Collection of Mr. and Mrs. Jack J. Katz.*

ROCKS AND TREES, MAINE. *1961. Oil. 50 x 40. Whitney Museum of American Art.*

STILL LIFE. *1962. Oil. 46 x 46. Collection of Lawrence H. Bloedel.*

MAINE LANDSCAPE. *1963. Oil. 50 x 52.*

BLACK ISLAND, MAINE. *1964. Oil. 46 x 50. Collection of Mr. and Mrs. Nathan R. Allen.*

MAINE INTERIOR. *1963. Oil. 50 x 50. Commerce Trust Company Collection, Kansas City, Mo.*

STILL LIFE WITH PEACHES AND BOTTLE. *1965. Oil. 16⅛ x 20. Collection of Susan and David Workman.*

SELF PORTRAIT IN INTERIOR. *1966. Oil. $49\frac{3}{4}$ x $48\frac{1}{4}$. Collection of Mr. and Mrs. John E. Shepherd.*

WOMAN AT DESK. *1966. Oil. 32⅜ x 36¼. Collection of Susan and David Workman.*

BOAT SHED — INTERIOR. *1967. Oil. 46 x 50. Collection of Francis J. Fabick.*

HARLEM RIVER LANDSCAPE. *1966-67. Oil. 39⅞ x 43⅞. Columbia University.*

COTTAGE INTERIOR. *1967. Oil. 60 x 50. Collection of Mrs. Eliot D. Pratt.*

EDGE OF THE ORCHARD. *1967. Oil. 46 x 52.*

STILL LIFE WITH GERANIUMS. *1967. Oil. 46 x 50. Collection of Susan and David Workman.*

CATALOGUE

The arrangement is chronological. The dimensions are in inches, height preceding width. All oils are either on canvas or masonite, and all watercolors and drawings on paper.

When no owner is given, the work is lent by the Kraushaar Galleries, New York.

OILS

1 INTERIOR. 1942. 23 x 31. Lent by Mr. and Mrs. Olin J. Stephens II.

2 SPRING LANDSCAPE. 1943. 25 x 30. Lent by Mr. and Mrs. Olin J. Stephens II. Il. p. 20.

3 MAINE COAST. 1944. 25 x 34. Lent by Atlanta University. Il. p. 22.

4 BOY IN WHITE. 1945. 28 x 21. Lent by George M. Moffett, Jr.

5 CLIFFS IN SHADOW. 1945. 24 x 36. Lent by Miss Dorothy C. Walker.

6 DRIFTWOOD. 1945. 40 x 30. Lent by Mr. and Mrs. Meyer P. Potamkin. Il. p. 21.

7 IMMERSION. 1947. $29\frac{1}{2}$ x $21\frac{1}{2}$. Lent by the New Britain Museum of American Art. Il. p. 23.

8 ROCKS AND DRIFTWOOD. 1947. 18 x 24. Lent by the New Britain Museum of American Art.

9 TARQUINIA. 1949. 15 x 25. Lent by Rosalie Berkowitz.

10 MONREALE. 1950. 28 x 22. Lent by the Philadelphia Museum of Art. Il. p. 24.

11 PALAZZO. 1951. 30 x 24. Lent by Mr. and Mrs. George S. Peer.

12 VENICE. 1950. 11 x $17\frac{1}{4}$. Lent by Mr. and Mrs. Alan H. Temple.

13 SAN SEPOLCRO. 1952. 24 x 15. Lent by the Wichita Art Museum, Roland P. Murdock Collection.

14 VIETRI. 1952. $12\frac{3}{4}$ x $19\frac{1}{2}$. Lent by Mr. and Mrs. Bernard Heineman, Jr.

15 OF MAINE. 1953. $15\frac{3}{4}$ x $28\frac{1}{2}$. Collection of the Whitney Museum of American Art. Il. p. 25.

16 EAST RIVER. 1954. 16 x 24. Lent by Mr. and Mrs. Olin J. Stephens II. Il. p. 28.

17 HARLEM RIVER. 1954. $12\frac{1}{2}$ x $25\frac{1}{4}$. Lent by Mr. and Mrs. Bernard Heineman, Jr. Il. p. 26.

18 INNSBRUCK. 1954. $17\frac{3}{4}$ x 11. Lent by the Memorial Art Gallery of the University of Rochester.

19 ROCKS. 1954. $22\frac{1}{2}$ x $11\frac{1}{2}$. Lent by William Bomar.

20 COURTYARD. 1955. $20\frac{1}{4}$ x $10\frac{3}{4}$. Lent by Mr. and Mrs. Jack J. Katz.

21 HIGH BRIDGE #2. 1955. $16\frac{3}{4}$ x $34\frac{1}{8}$. Lent by Mrs. Jules Enrich.

22 NOVA SCOTIA LANDSCAPE. 1955. 19 x $31\frac{3}{4}$.

23 WHITE ROCKS, NOVA SCOTIA. 1955. $13\frac{1}{2}$ x $24\frac{1}{2}$. Lent by Mrs. S. M. Barnes Roby. Il. p. 29.

24 FROM CRANBERRY ISLE. 1956. 30 x $40\frac{1}{4}$. Collection of the Whitney Museum of American Art.

25 STILL LIFE. 1956. $20\frac{5}{8}$ x $12\frac{1}{2}$. Lent by the Wadsworth Atheneum. Il. p. 27.

26 APPLE TREE. 1957. 25 x 40. Lent by the Rosenfield Collection, Des Moines Art Center.

27 CORINTHIAN LANDSCAPE. 1958. 32 x 46. Lent by Chauncey L. Waddell.

28 STILL LIFE. 1958. 40 x 30. Lent by M. Russell.

29 ISLAND LANDSCAPE. 1959. 46 x 46.
30 SELF PORTRAIT. 1959. 24 x 20. Lent by Armand G. Erpf. Frontispiece.
31 TOWARD THE ISLAND. 1959. 50 x 40. Lent by Atlanta University.
32 INTERIOR. 1961. 20 x 18¼. Lent by Mr. and Mrs. Jack J. Katz. Il. p. 30.
33 ROCKS AND TREES, MAINE. 1961. 50 x 40. Collection of the Whitney Museum of American Art, gift under the Ford Foundation Purchase Program. Il. p. 33.
34 STILL LIFE. 1962. 46 x 46. Lent by Lawrence H. Bloedel. Il. p. 32.
35 STILL LIFE WITH BOWL OF FRUIT. 1962. 20 x 24. Lent by Dr. and Mrs. Fletcher McDowell.
36 MAINE INTERIOR. 1963. 50 x 50. Lent by the Commerce Trust Company Collection, Kansas City, Mo. Il. p. 37.
37 MAINE LANDSCAPE. 1963. 50 x 52. Il. p. 34.
38 SELF PORTRAIT IN INTERIOR. 1963. 24 x 21. Lent by Mr. and Mrs. Charles Darwin Snelling.
39 BLACK ISLAND, MAINE. 1964. 46 x 50. Lent by Mr. and Mrs. Nathan R. Allen. Il. p. 35.
40 LANDSCAPE WITH TWO TREES. 1964. 12 x 17¾. Lent by Dr. Thomas A. Mathews.
41 STILL LIFE WITH LEMON. 1964. 26¼ x 26¼. Lent by Mr. and Mrs. Eliot D. Pratt.
42 COVE, LONG ISLAND, MAINE. 1965. 50 x 48. Lent by the Storm King Art Center.
43 HOWARD HOUSE. 1965. 50 x 52. Lent by the Sara Roby Foundation.
44 KITCHEN INTERIOR. 1965. 42 x 32. Lent by Mr. and Mrs. Morris Smoler. Il. p. 31.
45 KITCHEN TABLE. 1965. 35¾ x 40½. Lent by the J. B. Speed Art Museum.
46 STILL LIFE WITH PEACHES AND BOTTLE. 1965. 16⅛ x 20. Lent by Susan and David Workman. Il. p. 36.
47 BOATYARD AT THE POOL, CRANBERRY. 1966. 46½ x 50¼. Lent by the Northern Trust Company, Chicago.
48 INTERIOR — FROM THE LIVING ROOM. 1966. 40 x 38. Lent by the Museum of Art of Ogunquit.
49 INTERIOR WITH RED COUCH. 1966. 50½ x 50. Lent by Mr. and Mrs. Bob Schieffer.
50 SELF PORTRAIT IN INTERIOR. 1966. 49¾ x 48¼. Lent by Mr. and Mrs. John E. Shepherd. Il. p. 38.
51 SELF PORTRAIT, RED ROBE. 1966. 52 x 47. Lent by I. A. Weinstein.
52 WOMAN AT DESK. 1966. 32⅜ x 36¼. Lent by Susan and David Workman. Il. p. 39.
53 HARLEM RIVER LANDSCAPE. 1966-67. 39⅞ x 43⅞. Lent by Columbia University. Il. p. 40.
54 BOAT SHED — INTERIOR. 1967. 46 x 50. Lent by Francis J. Fabick. Il. p. 41.
55 BOY AT TABLE WITH CAT. 1967. 50 x 42.
56 CAT ON BEDSPREAD. 1967. 20 x 24.
57 COTTAGE INTERIOR. 1967. 60 x 50. Lent by Mrs. Eliot D. Pratt. Il. p. 43.
58 EARLY MORNING LANDSCAPE. 1967. 24¼ x 31.
59 EDGE OF THE ORCHARD. 1967. 46 x 52. Il. p. 42.
60 KITCHEN INTERIOR WITH FIGURE. 1967. 50 x 46.
61 STILL LIFE WITH GERANIUMS. 1967. 46 x 50. Lent by Susan and David Workman. Il. p. 44.

WATERCOLORS

The medium is watercolor unless otherwise stated.

62 STORMVILLE HILLS. 1936. 7¼ x 10¾. Ink and wash. Lent by the Nelson Gallery — Atkins Museum, gift of Maynard Walker.
63 STUDY 2. 1951. 18½ x 8⅝. Oil on paper. Lent by Rosalie Berkowitz.
64 STUDY. 1953. 20⅝ x 7½. Gouache. Lent by Mr. and Mrs. Alan L. Washburn. Il. p. 10.
65 ATTICA. 1957. 10 x 14. Lent by Mr. and Mrs. Martin Sumers.
66 FRUITS. 1962. 10¾ x 16¾. Wash. Lent by Mr. and Mrs. Robert Pesner.
67 TREES AND ROCKS. 1964. 12 x 7. Pencil and watercolor. Lent by Mr. and Mrs. Martin Sumers.
68 BLUE HILLS, MAINE. 1966. 8¾ x 13¼. Lent by Mr. and Mrs. Arthur Goldstone.
69 CENTRAL PARK LANDSCAPE. 1966. 8½ x 11½.
70 GIRL IN GREEN STRIPED DRESS. 1966. 13½ x 10¼. Watercolor and pastel. Lent by Mr. and Mrs. S. Deutsch.
71 STILL LIFE WITH FRUIT. 1966. 9 x 7. Lent by Mr. and Mrs. Robert Pesner.
72 STILL LIFE WITH RED JUG. 1966. 6 x 9. Lent by the artist.
73 BLUE CLOUD. 1967. 9 x 13⅝. Lent by Mr. and Mrs. Elliott M. Sanger.
74 LOW TIDE. 1967. 9 x 13. Lent by Malcolm R. McBride.
75 TREE. 1967. 13½ x 10⅝.

DRAWINGS

76 PIG STICKING. 1936. 9⅝ x 12. Ink. Lent by the University of Nebraska Art Galleries. Il. p. 7.
77 VERMONT AUCTION. 1943. 10¼ x 15. Ink. Lent by Mrs. John Sloan.
78 UNTITLED. 1945-46. 17¼ x 13½. Pastel.
79 CLIFFS. 1947. 11¼ x 16½. Ink. Lent by the Brooklyn Museum.
80 VOYAGE. 1948. 13½ x 21. Pastel. Il. p. 9.
81 STUDY. 1950. 15 x 23. Pastel and ink. Collection of the Whitney Museum of American Art.
82 SIENA. 1952. 14 x 20½. Ink and wash. Lent by Jane A. Mull.
83 NEAR DELPHI. 1957. 11 x 16. Ink. Lent by Mr. and Mrs. Martin Sumers.
84 #6 WITH RED AND ORANGE. 1957. 11 x 7½. Collage. Lent by Mr. and Mrs. Bernard Heineman, Jr.
85 END OF THE ISLAND, CRANBERRY. 1963. 13½ x 16¾. Ink. Lent by Henry Schnakenberg. Il. p. 11.
86 STILL LIFE. 1963. 23⅜ x 18⅞. Charcoal. Lent by Mr. and Mrs. Howard N. Berntsen. Il. p. 13.
87 STILL LIFE WITH SQUASH. 1966. 9 x 12. Red chalk. Lent by Mr. and Mrs. Lawrence Mark.
88 BOWL OF FRUIT. 1967. 13½ x 10½. Graphite pencil.
89 PORTRAIT. 1967. 23⅝ x 17⅜. Charcoal. Lent by Dr. and Mrs. William R. Shapiro.
90 PORTRAIT. 1967. 10 x 7½. Red chalk. Il. p. 15.

PRINTS

91 SELF PORTRAIT. 1963. 13 x 9½. Lithograph. Lent by Mr. and Mrs. Richard L. Wilkin.
92 STILL LIFE. 1963. 29 x 23. Lithograph. Lent by Mr. and Mrs. Richard L. Wilkin.
93 PORTRAIT OF C. 1967. 8⅞ x 6. Soft ground etching.
94 STILL LIFE. 1967. 4 x 5. Etching.

ACKNOWLEDGMENTS

This monograph is published on the occasion of the first full-scale retrospective exhibition of John Heliker's works, organized by the Whitney Museum of American Art in the spring of 1968.

The authors wish to express their great indebtedness to John Heliker for his cooperation in making his paintings and drawings available for study and exhibition, for furnishing full information about his life and work, and for discussing with us his ideas on art and his painting methods.

To Miss Antoinette Kraushaar of the Kraushaar Galleries, New York, which has represented the artist for twenty-seven years, and to Mrs. Robert Pesner of the Kraushaar Galleries, we wish to express our warm gratitude for their constant help throughout the planning of the exhibition.

We are also grateful for the assistance of Maynard Walker, who first exhibited the artist's work in the 1930's.

On behalf of the Whitney Museum of American Art we wish to thank the following museums and collectors whose generosity in lending works made the retrospective exhibition possible:

Atlanta University, Atlanta, Georgia; The Brooklyn Museum; Columbia University, New York; Commerce Trust Company Collection, Kansas City, Mo.; Des Moines Art Center, Des Moines, Iowa; The Memorial Art Gallery of the University of Rochester; Museum of Art of Ogunquit, Maine; Nelson Gallery — Atkins Museum, Kansas City, Mo.; The New Britain Museum of American Art, New Britain, Conn.; The Northern Trust Company, Chicago; Philadelphia Museum of Art; Sara Roby Foundation, New York; The J. B. Speed Art Museum, Louisville, Kentucky; Storm King Art Center, Mountainville, N.Y..; University of Nebraska Art Galleries, Lincoln; Wadsworth Atheneum, Hartford; Wichita Art Museum, Roland P. Murdock Collection, Wichita, Kansas.

Mr. and Mrs. Nathan R. Allen; Rosalie Berkowitz; Mr. and Mrs. Howard N. Berntsen; Lawrence H. Bloedel; William Bomar; Mr. and Mrs. S. Deutsch; Mrs. Jules Enrich; Armand G. Erpf; Francis J. Fabick; Mr. and Mrs. Arthur Goldstone; Mr. and Mrs. Bernard Heineman, Jr.; Mr. and Mrs. Jack J. Katz; Mr. and Mrs. Lawrence Mark; Dr. Thomas A. Mathews; Malcolm R. McBride; Dr. and Mrs. Fletcher McDowell; George M. Moffett, Jr.; Jane A. Mull; Mr. and Mrs. George S. Peer; Mr. and Mrs. Robert Pesner; Mr. and Mrs. Meyer P. Potamkin; Mr. and Mrs. Eliot D. Pratt; Mrs. S. M. Barnes Roby; M. Russell; Mr. and Mrs. Elliott M. Sanger; Mr. and Mrs. Bob Schieffer; Henry Schnakenberg; Dr. and Mrs. William R. Shapiro; Mr. and Mrs. John E. Shepherd; Mrs. John Sloan; Mr. and Mrs. Morris Smoler; Mr. and Mrs. Charles Darwin Snelling; Mr. and Mrs. Olin J. Stephens II; Mr. and Mrs. Martin Sumers; Mr. and Mrs. Alan H. Temple; Chauncey L. Waddell; Miss Dorothy C. Walker; Mr. and Mrs. Alan L. Washburn; I. A. Weinstein; Mr. and Mrs. Richard L. Wilkin; Susan and David Workman.